MILITARY MODEL SHOWCASE

BILL HORAN

Windrow & Greene

Printed in Singapore

This edition published in Great Britain by
Windrow & Greene Ltd.
19A Floral Street
London WC2E 9DS

Dedication
To my lovingly supportive wife Heather,
and her family, who still don't quite
know what to make of all this.

Photographic acknowledgements
Assembling the photographs and narrative material for
this book was a true pleasure, thanks to the support and
contributions of many talented people. I would like to
thank Mike Good, Derek Hansen, Martin Livingstone,
David Lock, Bill Ottinger, Sheperd Paine, Ron Tunison,
Peter Twist and Jean-Louis Viau of *Tradition* magazine
for contributing photographs. Most of all, thanks must
go to Nick Infield for his outstanding photographs, and
for his invaluable assistance in educating me in the
fascinating, if often frustrating world of miniature
photography. Unless specifically credited otherwise,
photographs are by the author.

(Cover photographs: **front,** "Attila the Hun" scratchbuilt
by Mike Good; **back,** "Trooper, Heavy Camel Regiment,
1885", scratchbuilt by Bill Horan using *Andrea Miniatures*
camel. Photos by Nick Infield and the author.)

A CIP catalogue record for this book is available from
the British Library.

ISBN 1-872004-28-8

STEADY HANDS, PATIENCE, AND A BRUSH WITH ONE HAIR

"They're so small!...Look at all that detail....You must use a magnifying glass....I can't even see it....I would never have the patience....You must have very steady hands....Do you use a brush with one hair?" There is probably not a modeller in the world who has not heard, in one language or another, at least a few of these exclamations from someone bending over to peer at their military miniatures for the first time. After a few years most miniaturists develop a standard response for each one whenever the topic comes up. Still, "a picture is worth a thousand words"; and the intent of this book is to provide about 100,000 words worth!

When most people see their first miniature military figure their reaction is usually one of astonishment. Most have never seen anything quite like it before; there are few art forms that combine so many artistic skills as miniature figure modelling. As with all creative endeavours, that of the military miniature has been blessed with some exceptionally talented artists whose work is both an inspiration to the aspiring modeller, and a challenge even to the experienced to strive for ever higher levels of achievement.

The term "military miniature" itself is really a misnomer, as many modellers focus their talents on purely non-military subjects. However, the term has become so commonly used throughout the world that I continue to employ it here, for simplicity. So what exactly is a military miniature? The basic definition is a miniature figure or group of figures realistically sculpted and painted to depict a specific military subject. The miniature can be a painted example of a mass-produced casting or "stock kit"; a "conversion" from parts of one or more such kits combined with a greater or lesser degree of original handwork; entirely "scratchbuilt"; or a vignette/diorama. Within these categories are many variations including busts, flats, and fantasy (science fiction) miniatures, among others.

Miniatures also come in a wide variety of sizes, ranging from the ubiquitous 54mm scale (giving a human figure about 2 1/4 inches tall) to the normal upper limit of 120mm (about 5 1/2 inches), by way of the now popular 90mm (3 1/2-inch) scale. Readers should always bear in mind, as they study the photographs in this book, that *most of the figures they are looking at are no taller than a cigarette.* Even the experienced eye can often be seduced into forgetting this remarkable fact by the sheer craft that goes into these miniature masterpieces. All require painting skill; and the more complex forms demand considerably more than that. Sculpting, engineering,

historical research, an eye for composition, landscape design, even electrical wiring and lighting design come together in various combinations to form a truly unique artistic creation: the miniature painted figure or diorama.

This book showcases some of the best military miniatures produced over the past fifteen years, including work by many of the most acclaimed masters. During the past ten years I have regularly attended exhibitions and competitions on both sides of the Atlantic, and the quality of military miniature art has never ceased to inspire and fascinate me. I hope the reader enjoys these outstanding miniatures as much as I have.

Buena Park, California, June 1992

"Colour-Sergeant, Grenadier Guards, 1914", designed and painted by **David Grieve.** (Photo: Derek Hansen)

1: THE FIGURE PAINTERS
Painting the "Stock" Figure

There is no skill so essential to the successful miniaturist as the ability to paint well. The most brilliantly detailed kit, the most ingeniously modified conversion, the most magnificently crafted "scratchbuilt" figure, even the most breathtakingly conceived and composed diorama can be fatally flawed by mediocre painting. The one common thread that links all successful miniature art is good painting. Painting is outwardly the most immediately discernible feature of every miniature, and as such makes the first impression on the viewer – the "make or break" impression which can never be fully retrieved by the more lengthy examination which may reveal merits not accessible to the first glance. While many miniaturists were drawn to their hobby by a desire to paint model figures, many others take for granted just how central good painting is to the challenge of creating a memorable miniature figure or scene. The best modellers never forget this, and continue to develop and improve their painting skills even as other aspects of their modelling abilities evolve.

Left:
Departing from his favourite Victorian era, **John Canning** could not resist trying his hand at *Poste Militaire's* "Mameluke" – a particularly well animated and detailed figure designed by Julian Hullis.(Photo:Nick Infield)

Opposite top & bottom:
There are few painters comparable to **Greg DiFranco** and England's **Derek Hansen,** as these pictures show; we have deliberately chosen subjects which do not distract by any immediately dramatic appearance. Greg's rendition of *Chota Sahib's* "Daffadar, Madras Lancers" captures the details such as campaign medals and turban pattern with crisp precision, while the varying shades of subtle colour in, for instance, the blues of the different parts of the uniform are convincingly rendered. The *Hornet Miniatures* "Desert Rat" is a simple yet wonderfully lifelike figure designed by Roger Saunders which Derek Hansen has taken to an even higher level by near-perfect painting. Note the strongly individual character imparted by the exquisitely detailed face; and the many subtle shadow and highlight tones in the apparently simple khaki drill shirt and shorts. These quiet masterpieces show two outstanding painters at their best.

Painting is a subject upon which virtually everyone associated with military miniatures considers himself an expert, capable of selecting with absolute certainty the best-painted pieces in any exhibition. In a way, of course, everyone *is* an expert in the sense that he knows what he likes: no two people have exactly the same perception of what constitutes good painting, but almost everyone seems to know it when they see it. In the most general terms, what people like in miniature painting is realism. The more realistically painted a piece is, the more attention and praise it is likely to attract. Abstract expressionism, surrealism and impressionism may enjoy a strong and well-deserved following in the art world as a whole, but at the miniature level realism still rules.

What fascinates me most about figure painting is the diversity of styles, mediums and techniques employed by the world's modellers, all of which can succeed beautifully. Most painters rely on artist oil colours, including such well-known exponents as Derek Hansen, Greg DiFranco, Phil Kessling and Brian Stewart. The slow drying time - allowing subtle blending techniques - and wide range of vibrant colours make oil paints an almost irresistible choice for figure painters. However, a few have remained

stubbornly loyal to the enamel paints which they probably first used when painting plastic model aircraft or tank kits in a "previous chapter" of their modelling life. Mike Good, Mike Leonard, Adrian Bay, John Bernier and the author are among this group of diehards, for whom the dead flat finish and the precision of enamels make them trusted allies. Fewer still (one thinks of David Grieve and Jim Hill) use water-based paints - plakas and acrylics - for the sake of their bright colours and reliable clarity.

Of course, the best painters will say that the medium chosen is really unimportant. What matters is how well one is able to overcome a medium's weaknesses and build on its strengths - for they all do have particular weaknesses and strengths. Oil paints tend to dry to finishes ranging from matt to high gloss - a fact that causes oil painters particular frustration when painting dark blue and green clothing. Enamels dry in between 20 and 30 minutes - too fast for the typically methodical painter - and come in a rather drab assortment of colours. Water-based paints dry instantly, however, thus making any patient, subtle blending of adjacent shades almost impossible. Somehow good painters manage to overcome these difficulties and develop techniques so carefully honed that their results make painting seem almost...simple. Bite your tongue! There's nothing simple about it.

Below:
Long considered one of the best "pure" painters in North America, Canadian miniaturist **Francisco (Frank) Fernandez** tackled a rarely seen *Series 77* kit - "Moghul Cavalryman". A remarkably prolific and skilful painter, Frank is best known for his superbly painted mounted figures. Here two contrasting challenges are obvious: the difficult access to the eyes almost hidden back inside the helmet, a problem which all too often leads to an overlarge, staring effect; and the soft subtlety of large areas of animal hide unbroken by specific surface details. Frank has overcome both challenges with masterly skill.

Opposite:
Never entered in competition, the author's painting of *Tiny Troopers'* 90mm "Colonel Douglas, 11th Hussars, 1856" highlights the sculpting skills of designer Mike French to good advantage. Painting metallic braid often presents a problem; here, dark browns were added to the gold to deepen the colour of the braid, creating a richer finish which contrasts with the bright gilt buttons.

Above:
Although rarely seen on the miniature "show circuit", Californian **Jim Hill** earned silver medals at several competitions with his "Union Drummer", a 54mm *Taxdir* kit. Again, the apparent simplicity of large, almost unbroken areas of ostensibly "single" colours is deceptive; to achieve a controlled effect like this takes skill and experience.

Above & right:
Jerry Hutter and **Phil
Kessling** have consistently
earned gold medals with
their impressively painted *Le
Cimier* 54mm Napoleonics.
Jerry collected a silver medal
at the 1989 Euro-Militaire
competition with his
"French Line Infantry
Officer"; while the Polish
chic of "General Krasinski"
well illustrates Phil's painting
and presentation skills.

Top right:
Mike Leonard has won numerous awards for his conversion work, which earned him the title "Grand Master" at the MFCA competition in the 1970s. Mike's enamel-painted Great War "Zeppelin Commander", a *Hecker & Goros* figure, is presented with an imaginative sympathy for the period and subject.

Below:
A relative newcomer to the "show circuit", Florida's **Keith Kawalski** turned heads with his "Officer, City of London Volunteers", one of Sid Horton's characteristically clean *Chota Sahib* figures. Again, this 54mm miniature is finished not only with technical skill,

but with a real sympathy for individual character.
(Photo:Nick Infield)

Bottom right:
Californian **Chuck Smith** departed from his well-known "flat" painting to take on *Almond Sculptures'* 18th century "Prussian Hussar Officer"; Chuck's fine work is mostly seen at the California (SCAMMS) Show.(Photo:Nick Infield)

Above:
No one can surpass **Brian Stewart's** ability to capture the soldier's physical environment; but those who follow Brian's work know that his skills don't stop with the groundwork. Note the convincingly worn look he has painted into *Poste Militaire's* early 16th century "English Halberdier", a 70mm kit designed by Keith Durham. The overall impression is one of complete harmony between the soldier and the muddy heather of his Border battlefield. Less experienced modellers can fail to achieve this visual consistency even though figure and groundwork may be individually well-finished.

Top right:
France's **Dominique Breffort** is known in Europe for his association with *Tradition* magazine, for which he regularly writes articles on aspects of the military miniaturist's art. His well-painted Peninsular War "British Officer, 1812" is a 54mm kit by *Beneito*.

Right:
Steven Weakley turned in a first rate painting of *Poste Militaire's* "Attila the Hun", an 80m kit designed by fellow Californian Mike Good. (Photo:Nick Infield)

Left:
Welsh modeller **Gary Joslyn** earned a gold medal at the 1992 Euro-Militaire competiton for his Second World War tank officer of the 17th/21st Lancers in North-West Europe. (Photo:David Lock)

Bottom left:
The intense cold and deprivation of the Russian winter, 1942-43, are vividly reflected in the pinched face of this *Little Generals* kit, "German Infantryman", superbly painted by **Jim Ryan**. Jim collected a silver medal for his collection of painted stock figures at the 1992 MFCA Show.

Below:
MFCA Grand Master and Chicago Medallist **Joe Berton**, in addition to being an expert on Middle Eastern history, is also an exceptionally talented modeller and painter. History and art combined when Joe painted *Andrea Miniatures'* 54mm "Lawrence of Arabia" – a subject particularly close to his heart. The painting of the intricately woven camel blanket and bags was accomplished with notable skill.

FOCUS ON FLATS

"Flat" painting has been an important specialised branch of the military miniature art for many years, originally having strong associations with Germany; it is a particularly demanding field, attracting some of the most talented painters in the world. "Flats" are white metal castings which are essentially flat, being only about 3/16 in. thick and ranging from 30mm to 90mm in height, both sides of the casting being sculpted in low relief. The key to successful flat painting is the selection of a specific perceived light source, meaning that shadows and other aspects of more conventional "canvas" painting must be convincingly and consistently rendered.

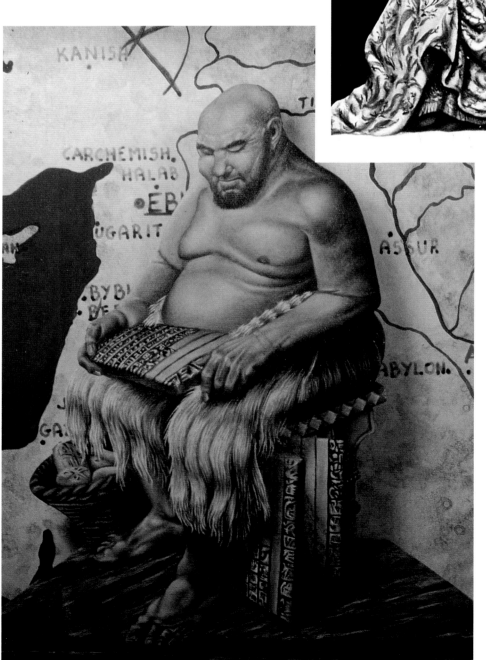

Above:
Well-known English flat painter **Mike Taylor** collected gold medals at Euro- Militaire and Chicago for his exquisite little "Madame de Pompadour". (Photo: Nick Infield)

Left:
R.Ramakers' stunningly painted "The Scribe, 2,300 BC" garnered a gold medal at the 1989 Euro-Militaire competition.

14

American Grand Master
Greg DiFranco's
outstanding "Kaiser
Maximilian" (below) dazzled
spectators at the 1992 MFCA
Show. Greg's superb boxed
flat scene **"L'Empereur"**
(left) brought him a gold
medal and Best of Show at
Chicago in 1989.

2: THE CONVERTERS
Transforming a Figure

There is no term that encompasses so much in the world of the military miniature as the word "conversion". Technically, the meaning is simple: to modify an existing commercially available cast figure into something different - but the term conceals an astonishingly wide range of ambition and skill. It can be applied to an existing kit figure to which the most insignificant changes have been made, such as the substitution of a sword for a spear, or even the addition of a moustache. It is also used to describe figures that are virtually built "from scratch" with the exception of a few commercially available accessories, such as a rifle or a pair of hands. Between these two extremes lies a limitless variety of conversion projects.

In years past the availability of commercially supplied accessories (i.e. "spare parts" available as separate castings, rather than parts sawn off complete figures condemned to cannibalisation) was more or less limited to the French Napoleonic *Historex* range of plastic components. Modellers wishing to depict soldiers of most other historical periods were left with little choice but to build them from scratch. Sheperd Paine and Peter Twist are typical of the 1970s miniaturists who jumped from *Historex* conversions to scratchbuilding. However, the 1980s and 1990s have seen a flood of miniature figure accessories arrive on the market to cater for almost any modeller's individual vision. Manufacturers such as *Hornet, Puchala, Scale Link, Andrea* and particularly the ubiquitous *Verlinden* have made available to the modeller a treasure trove of accessories, from rifles and swords to horses and camels, from heads and hands to boots and crates - even minute, delicately photo-etched sheet brass badges, ears and eyeglasses! The miniaturist wishing to create a unique figure can now do so far more easily than ever before. For this reason the art of conversion has seen something of a renaissance.

The converted figures illustrated in the following pages reflect the ingenuity typical of the world's top miniaturists. The vast majority of conversions showcased here are in 54mm, a scale of enduring popularity in which most of the lines of commercial accessories are supplied. *Historex* continues to be very popular, particularly in the area of mounted figures; and modellers such as Martin Livingstone, Bill Ottinger and Keith Engledow have ably carried the torch passed on by the great *Historex* masters of the 1970s.

Many talented miniaturists have shown that ambitious conversions are possible in many other scales, notably Brian Stewart and Peter Wilcox, both of whom have dazzled spectators with their extensively converted 80mm *Sovereign* figures. Jim Johnston has also come up with several cleverly transformed 100mm and 120mm figures, including one illustrated in this chapter. Using a wide assortment of epoxy

During the 1970s and early 1980s English modeller Graham Bickerton was a leader in the art of the *Historex* conversion. Graham reappeared at Euro-Militaire in 1989, winning plaudits for his French Napoleonic artillery officer, whimsically entitled "A Bridge Too Short". The sense of rapid movement abruptly halted, in both horse and rider, is particularly well conveyed.

putties, sheet plastic, lead, copper, paper, wire - even electrician's tape - converters are creating some of the most exciting and innovative work now appearing at miniature exhibitions around the world. Miniaturists seem to get a tremendous amount of pleasure from seeing a good conversion, and working out in their minds just what was taken from the kit and what was scratchbuilt. There is a very specific look that comes over a modeller's face when he sees a particularly good conversion for the first time: it seems to be saying,"What a great idea...why didn't I think of that?"

Above:
Combining a variety of
Historex components with a
healthy dose of
scratchbuilding, **Greg
DiFranco's** immaculate
"Major, 6th Regiment
Chevau-Legers, 1812" took a
gold medal at the 1990
Chicago Show.

Top right:
Jean-Pierre Duthilleul is
one of France's leading
modellers, and his nearly
scratchbuilt conversion "The
Pasha" won a first place at the
1991 Sevres competition.
Note the beautifully designed
and painted room setting.
(Photo:Jean-Louis Viau)

Right:
Although his output is small,
Florida's **Scott Eble** has
recently been impressing
judges and spectators alike
with his conversion and
painting abilities. His "SS-
Obersturmfuhrer" earned him
gold medals at the Atlanta,
California and MFCA shows
in 1992. (Photo:Nick Infield)

Right:
Jerry Hutter's first converted figure, this strongly individual "French Officer of the Line, 1800", earned him gold at the 1990 Chicago Show. Few commercial parts were used, most of the figure being scratchbuilt; the tricorn brim was fashioned by rolling out A & B putty.

Left:
Flamboyance and a talent for painting intricate detail are key elements in the work of English modeller **Keith Engledow.** His extensively converted mounted piece "The Mongol" demonstrates the flair that can make a figure stand out.

Right:
Jim Johnston's remarkable
transformation of *Verlinden's*
"General Schwarzkopf"
figure into the late medieval
Polish prince "Janusz
Radziwill" was accomplished
with a load of A & B putty
and a great deal of
imagination and skill. The
pearly finish so beautifully
achieved on the silk tunic was
realised with an additional
coat of a special translucent
paint.(Photo:Nick Infield)

Below:
Often a relatively simple change to a good commercial kit can make it even more dynamic: **Phil Kessling** substituted a highly animated *Verlinden* head for that of a *D.F.Grieve* kit, "Sergeant, 66th (Berkshire) Regiment, 1880". This hero of Maiwand earned Phil a gold medal at Chicago in 1990.

Right:
Another good example of an excellent conversion, based on little more than the armature of a kit is **Bob Knee's** "Russian Sniper" of the Great Patriotic War, complete with scratchbuilt camouflage suit, cap and converted Mosin-Nagant rifle.

Opposite top:
Sheperd Paine modified *Series 77's* "Corporal, U.S.Dragoons, 1844" by lengthening the legs to add height – and elegance. The willingness and ability to make such a fundamental but challenging modification for the sake of that last ten per cent of visual appeal sets the serious miniaturist apart.

Opposite bottom:
At the 1983 MFCA Show **Andrei Koribanics** drew a large crowd around his exhibit. The attraction was his marvellously romanticised "Bonaparte", a gold medal winner for this talented Grand Master. The body and head were reworked from *Historex* components, and the blowing greatcoat skirts were skilfully fashioned from sheet aluminium.

Opposite right:
Mike Stelzel first showed this unique conversion – "Officer, 2nd Life Guards, 1885" – at the 1991 MFCA Show, where it earned him a gold medal. He had replaced the original head with a *Verlinden* accessory - on a figure that *he* had sculpted!

ADRIAN BAY (ENGLAND)

In recent years those attending the BMSS Annuals and Euro-Militaire have noticed the steady rise of a skilled young London modeller, Adrian Bay. Making extensive use of *Airfix "Multipose"* kits, commercially available accessories, and a good deal of imagination, Adrian has earned gold and silver medals at these two major British competitions as well as a gold at the California Show in 1992. His painting style is notable for the exclusive use of enamel paints, which bring a crispness and precision to his figures. He has even mastered the universally dreaded tartan and chequers, by the skilful use of subdued colours and a very steady hand: study here his leaping Celt, and always remember - the whole figure is only as tall as a cigarette....In addition to his artistic skills Adrian is considered an expert on the British cavalry of the Crimean War, a fact which frequently suggests his choice of subjects. Illustrated here are his models of "Adrianix the Celt"; "Capitaine Dampierre, 1854"; and (opposite) "Sergeant Ramage, VC, Scots Greys, 1854" - the latter photographed by Nick Infield.

BILL HORAN (U.S.A.)

A selection of figures by the author. The "Drummer, Grenadier Guards, 1854" was virtually scratchbuilt, the drum and drumsticks *(Historex)* and the head (modified *Airfix*) being the only commercial items used. The heads, sword and rifle are the only commercial castings used in the "Officer, 72nd Highlanders, 1858" and "Private, 146th New York Volunteer Infantry, 1864". The balance of both figures was sculpted with A & B and Duro epoxy putties; and all were painted in enamels.

24

BILL OTTINGER (U.S.A.)

Like Graham Bickerton's, Bill Ottinger's work reflects an affection for the Napoleonic soldier in all his colour and splendour. *Historex* conversions are his speciality, and few can match his expertise in this area. Bill is one of the most enthusiastic miniaturists in the United States, and eagerly shares his many innovations in *Historex* conversion techniques with aspiring imitators. Bill's work has attracted major awards at shows in Atlanta, Philadelphia and Chicago, where he received the Chicago Medal in 1989. We show here his models of a "General, French Cuirassiers, 1812", which seems to capture perfectly the blunt determination of that generation of French officers of humble background who won their stars young on the battlefields of the new Empire; and, saluting with his sabre, an "Officer, Light Horse of Berg" glowing in white and rose.

BRIAN STEWART (U.S.A.)

Brian Stewart is one of the truly unique talents working today in the military miniature field. He continually demonstrates an ability to portray convincingly a wide variety of landscapes, walls, buildings, rubble - even interesting dirt! Brian's groundwork skills add an extra dimension to his work. His favourite historical period is the ancient world, and extensively converted *Sovereign* figures have become his trademark. Brian relies principally upon A & B putty for his conversions and scratchbuilding. His efforts have made him a virtual sure bet for a gold medal in any competition he enters, including Euro-Militaire in 1988 and numerous triumphs at the Chicago, MFCA and California Shows, where he has been honoured with the title Master for sustained excellence. Brian is now employed by *Kirin Miniatures* as a figure designer, and he should continue to have an important influence on the work of miniaturists for years to come. Illustrated here are his "Burgundian Warrior", crowned with a wild boar mask and set in typically meticulous scenery; a brooding "Germanic Warrior, lst Century AD"; and **(overleaf)** a wonderfully defiant, bronze-helmeted "Gallic Warrior".

DEREK HANSEN (ENGLAND)

Since 1988, when he collected his first gold medal at Euro-Militaire, well-deserved awards have rained down on Derek Hansen. Whether painted stock figures, conversions or scratchbuilts, Derek has consistently exhibited work of the highest quality. The two figures illustrated here (in his own photographs) are typical of his conversion techniques. The "German Landsturm Battalion Nr.58, 1915" is converted from a modern *Hornet* figure with extensively reworked and scratchbuilt items added, notably the shako and equipment. Derek's spectacular "Trooper, 5th Westphalian Uhlans, 1915" was based on the *Andrea Miniatures* kit, with over 50 per cent of the horse and rider built from scratch. Both brought Derek awards, the mounted Uhlan winning Best of Show at Euro-Militaire in 1990. His painting style may be unique among miniaturists: he uses a layering/wash technique with oil paints which creates a very subtle, lifelike effect. He is now heavily involved in producing masters for *Poste Militaire,* and his work promises to remain in the forefront of the hobby for years to come.

Opposite:
Brian Stewart's "Gallic Warrior".

MARTIN LIVINGSTONE (ENGLAND)

For several years Martin has been among the most frequently honoured modellers in Britain, collecting gold medals at the BMSS Annuals and Euro-Militaire, and Best of Show at the 1991 Sevres competition in France. His most recognizable work is based on *Historex* components supplemented by Milliput modifications. His striking "Gallic Chieftain, 3rd Century BC" is illustrated here, together with his converted *Hornet Miniatures* kit "SS-Division No.12 'Hitlerjugend', 1944", in his own photographs; Martin takes special pleasure in the diversity of subjects that appeal to him.

PETER WILCOX (ENGLAND)

Fascination with the ancient world is also a dominant theme in the work of veteran Peter Wilcox. Like his American counterpart Brian Stewart, Peter makes the most of John Tassel's 80mm *Sovereign Miniatures* as a solid foundation for his extensive conversions, but many of his figures are so heavily modified as to be virtual scratchbuilts. Peter takes justifiable pride in the time and care that go into each

one of his masterpieces, particularly the intricately painted patterned clothing seen on many of them. It shows....His subjects here are a "Gallic Warrior, 3rd Century" contemplating a beautifully painted shield; a "Gallic Assault Leader, 2nd Century"; and the mounted "Western Sarmatian (Alan), 8th Century" which won him another gold medal at Euro–Militaire in 1991. (Photos:Derek Hansen)

3: THE SCRATCHBUILDERS
Building a Figure from the Ground Up

Creating a figure "from scratch" - the modeller sculpting the entire figure - is one of the miniaturist's greatest challenges. While many have tinkered with conversions, even going so far as to scratchbuild clothing and equipment for a figure, the daunting prospect of creating a convincing miniature anatomy complete with lifelike face, hands, weapons, shoes (or even worse, bare feet) is enough to strike fear into the heart of even the most determined modeller. Before the boom in accessory part sales scratchbuilding was the only way for a modeller to recreate figures outside the mainstream of subjects. However, as "spare parts" have become more plentiful, so scratchbuilding has come into its own; and many masters of this art are now working as figure designers for major kit manufacturers. Mike Good, Derek Hansen, Michel Saez, Andre Bleskine, Bruno Leibovitz, Bill Merklein, David Grieve, Peter Twist and Ron Tunison are among the better-known scratchbuilders now sculpting commercially.

Sculptors will freely admit that creating masters for casting and kit production is a very different task from sculpting one-of-a-kind figures. The engineering which has to go into designing a figure that can be successfully removed from a mold after hardening can severely limit its degree of animation. The more exaggerated the pose, the more difficult it can be to cast successfully, requiring it to be broken down into more and more sub-components, each of which may suffer shrinkage and distortion during the molding process. Commercially designed figures therefore tend to be standing characters in relatively relaxed poses, the more animated "action" poses being generally confined to "one-offs" and conversions.

How do they do it? The most common method used today is for a modeller to first create a standard armature of upper and lower torso, head, hands (probably without fingers at this stage) and feet. These parts are then attached to one another with a heavy wire, creating a "stick figure" which can then be manipulated into the desired pose. The "flesh" of the limbs, the clothing and other details are then sculpted, using a two-part epoxy putty. The choice of putties is important, and regional preferences seem to have developed.

European modellers continue to rely on Milliput, a white putty that can be carved easily when dry. North American miniaturists rely on two types of putty: A & B, and Duro. The former is a very soft medium when first mixed, and is generally smoothed and contoured with a brush and water as it sets, since it eventually dries to a rock-hard finish that is very difficult to carve. Duro is a very smooth, waxy substance, making it ideal for fine detail and clothing folds, though a bit too stiff to portray drapery convincingly. A few modellers use a substance called "Sculpey", a more traditional sculpting clay

which is baked to harden it. As miniaturists on either side of the Atlantic exchange ideas and techniques there has been some interpenetration of the two styles, but not much. Whatever the substance chosen, the results achieved by these talented artists are very impressive indeed, proving once again that it is neither medium nor technique that makes the piece, but the skill of the technician.

Left:
Derek Hansen earned a gold medal at the 1991 Chicago Show for his excellent "Prussian Uhlan", now a popular *Poste Militaire* kit. Derek *likes* Uhlans... (Photo: Nick Infield)

Below:
Standing over 12 inches in height, this Napoleonic "Colonel, 8th Regiment of Cuirassiers" by renowned French artist **Charles Conrad** is a dazzling piece of modelling brilliance. The cuirass, sabre and helmet are fashioned from metal, and the figure is dressed in specially tailored scale clothing. Skilful painting, sculpting and tailoring make this a uniquely impressive piece. (Photo: Jean-Louis Viau)

Previous page:
The casual elegance of this "Officer of Russian Guard Cavalry" is a striking tribute to the sculpting skill of Russian artist **Andre Bleskine.** (Photo: Jean-Louis Viau)

Right:
Jim Holt is a relative newcomer to the ranks of scratchbuilders, but his "Troop Sergeant-Major, 11th Hussars, 1854" impressed visitors and judges alike at the 1992 California Show, and won him a gold medal.

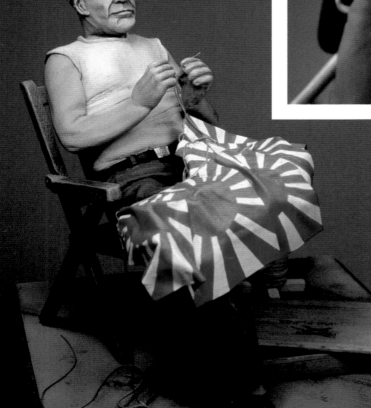

Left:
Kim Jones of Tulsa, Oklahoma has a real affinity for the American serviceman, as demonstrated by his wonderfully expressive "U.S. Sailor, 1944". It takes real familiarity with a subject to come up with the idea for an unusual, undramatic but entirely characteristic pose like this: something special to the human type, the service and the period.

Below:
There is probably no modeller more skilled at capturing the horseman in motion than France's **Jean Josseau.** His "Mameluke", astride a beautiful and beautifully rendered Arabian steed, is typical of the dynamic movement so effectively captured in Jean's work. (Photo: Jean-Louis Viau)

Right:
One of the most respected commercial figure designers today is English artist **Julian Hullis.** His 120mm masters designed for *Verlinden* and *Poste Militaire* are wildly popular with modellers, and are seen in impressive numbers at exhibitions around the world. In 1991 Julian added another feather to his cap, receiving Best of Show at Euro-Militaire for his outstanding Mongol archer "Watching the Steppes". Note the extraordinary quality of, for instance, the hands; and also the beautifully controlled textures of the different painted surfaces. (Photo: David Lock)

Below:
Perhaps the best-known and most admired modeller in France is **Bruno Leibovitz,** the principal sculptor for *Le Cimier* 54mm figures and creator of the *Metal Modeles* line. Many modellers may be unaware, however, of the one-of-a-kind figures which Bruno has produced over the years, including this immaculate "Baron Desvaux de Saint Maurice". (Photo: Jean-Louis Viau)

Right:
Bill Merklein is one of the most versatile sculptors in the United States. His credits include not only many miniatures for *Battleline* and *Le Cimier,* but also range from the "GI Joe"/"Action Man" masters, to the dove for the Visa card hologram! Bill's 12-inch "Confederate Infantryman" is illustrated here.

Right:
Large scale Native Americans are the primary focus of **Bob Murphy's** work. His colourful "Buffalo Bill's Totem" was a popular gold medal winner at the 1989 MFCA Show. Large areas of unclothed flesh and animal hide demand great sculpting and painting skills.

"*One of Jeb's Boys* "
RON TUNISON

Left & opposite top:
The American soldier is
depicted with drama and
accuracy by professional
sculptor and painter **Ron
Tunison.** Ron is best
known for his American Civil
War subjects, such as his
superb Confederate Cavalry
figure entitled "One of Jeb's
Boys". However, this
talented member of the
Company of Military
Historians and the Society of

American Historical Artists is equally adept at depicting the American frontier, as can be seen from his exquisite 7th Cavalryman on the Plains, entitled "Dawn Attack". Ron's list of achievements includes a bronze statue of General Crawford of the Pennsylvania Reserves which now stands in the "Valley of Death" on the Gettysburg battlefield. (Photos: Ron Tunison)

39

MIKE GOOD (U.S.A.)

Since attending his first major military miniature exhibition in the early 1980s California modeller **Mike Good** has become one of the most talented and well-known miniaturists in the world. Sculpted from a wide range of epoxy putties, Mike's scratchbuilt figures have won many major awards: in fact, since 1983 he has won at least one gold medal at *every* show he has attended. At Euro-Militaire in 1988 his craggy-faced "Hanoverian Artillery Train Driver" was honoured with a gold medal and Best of Show. Since then Mike has devoted an increasing part of his time to the creation of master sculptures for *Poste Militaire, Le Cimier,* and most recently *Kirin Miniatures.* Also shown here, magnificently photographed by Nick Infield, is Mike's award-winning "Attila the Hun", upon which his *Poste Militaire* kit was based. British Great War ace-of-aces "Mick Mannock" is an earlier scratchbuilt 80mm figure - a gold medal winner at the California and MFCA Shows.

DAVID GRIEVE (ENGLAND)

The work of miniature artist **David Grieve** is known to modellers throughout the world, who have been buying and painting his *D.F.Grieve* 65mm and 100mm kits for more than ten years now. David creates his figures using a two-step process, the first involving the sculpture of the basic figure in a wax/plasticene compound. The second step comes after the basic figure has been cast in white metal, at which point details are sharpened and solder, brass and copper are used to add belts, cords, and other fine touches. While the outstanding quality of David's sculpting

may be no secret, fewer modellers may know of his formidable painting skill. Using water-based Plaka paints, a medium which allows virtually no blending time due to its fast-drying nature, David has developed a very clean, precise style which does full justice to the details he strives so hard to reproduce in the sculpting and casting of his figures. These photographs show David's "Grenadier Guardsman, Camel Corps, 1885"; and "Senior Drum Major, Household Division, 1990" – a 140mm figure produced to celebrate the tenth anniversary of D.F.Grieve Models.

PETER TWIST (CANADA)

For the past fifteen years **Peter Twist** has been one of the most influential miniaturists in North America. Although he has won much acclaim for his vignettes and box dioramas, Peter is best known for his outstanding 90mm scratchbuilt figures. Working primarily in A & B putty, he has developed a very clean sculpting style that is complimented by his precise, colourful oil painting technique. Peter has a wide range of historical interests, as can be seen from the small selection illustrated here: a 17th century "Polish Winged Hussar"; a French Napoleonic cuirassier in Russia, 1812, "Defiant" though unhorsed; a close-up of his wounded "Private, lst Royal Dragoons, 1812"; and **(overleaf)** his wonderfully poignant "Joan of Arc". Armour can be portrayed with remarkable authenticity by polishing the cast metal with steel wool and buffing with a soft cloth; some modellers swear by the effect of burnishing with a suitable metal tool.
(Photos: Peter Twist)

BUSTS

Right top & bottom:
The sculpting of busts is, of course, an ancient tradition in the world of art; but their introduction into the mainstream of the military miniature hobby is relatively new, and welcome. Today several miniaturists are doing their most creative work in this new field, where the mercilessly large scale challenges the master sculptor and painter to really show off his skills. **Mike Good** has consistently turned out first rate "character" busts, typically depicting unusual subjects. This "Jivaro" was one of three Mike completed in 1988 devoted to headhunting tribes of the 19th century; less obscure but no less impressive was his "Buffalo Soldier" - a private of the 9th U.S.Cavalry, 1880, which received a gold medal at Euro-Militaire in 1989.

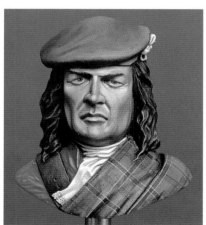

Above top & bottom:
Chris Walther of Memphis, Tennessee is another American modeller best known for his fascinating and beautifully executed busts; his "Zulu" warrior was part of his gold medal winning exhibit at the 1990 Chicago Show. There are few bust castings commercially available, but one such is **Gary Dombrowski's** "Jacobite", masterfully painted here (and photographed) by Derek Hansen.

45

MICHEL SAEZ (FRANCE)

Perhaps one of the most interesting aspects of the military miniature hobby is the recurring theme of a talented modeller developing an amazing empathy for the soldiers of another country. Despite the rich military heritage of his native France, **Michel Saez** has become fascinated by the British Victorian era; he has focused his sculpting and painting skills on personalities of that period, and has chosen busts as his canvas. Working exclusively in Milliput, Michel is, by his own admission, a very slow worker, but the results speak for themselves. Michel is now also working closely with Bruno Leibovitz of *Metal Modeles* as a figure designer, so his 54mm Napoleonic figures should continue to grace the hobby; but to those who appreciate the combination of outstanding sculpting and painting Michel's busts will continue to be a favourite and distinctive byway within the hobby. Here we feature his "Private, 95th Foot, 1854"; "Officer, 93rd Highlanders, 1854" (photo: Nick Infield); and "Chasseur d'Afrique, 1854" (photo: Jean-Louis Viau).

FANTASY

The plight of non-military subjects in the world of the miniature is sometimes a sad one. Although "fantasy" work is regarded as on equal terms with military modelling in France and the U.S.A., in some other countries fantasy pieces are considered as "outsiders", not to be taken seriously by modellers of historical reality. This is a pity, given the often remarkable skills applied to subjects which, by definition, may require quite extreme "special effects". Euro-Militaire has recently established a category for the exhibition of fantasy work, giving British and visiting modellers a major competition forum in which to display their skills.

There is certainly no shortage of impressively modelled work in the non-military field these days. **Mike Good** came close to winning Best of Show at the MFCA and California Shows in 1991 and 1992 respectively with his brilliantly painted 12-inch kit "Nosferatu", seen here in his own photograph.

The 1992 California Show's top honours eventually went to **John Rosengrant** for his brilliant scratchbuilt bust of Arnold Schwarzenegger's character from the film *"Terminator 2"*. John had worked on the film's model crew, and was mentioned in the internationally televised Oscar ceremony for his contribution to the award-winning special make-up effects. "Terminator" was first sculpted, then chrome-plated to give realism to the android's metallic inner skull. Note the lifelike texture of the skin, and the baleful glow of the red grain-of-wheat bulb incorporated in the eye.(Photo: Nick Infield)

4: VIGNETTES & DIORAMAS
Telling a Story

In the vignette and the diorama all elements of military miniature art come together, with another universally appealing element - a story. Vignettes and dioramas are arguably the greatest achievements of the miniaturist's art, and are consistently the most popular pieces at any exhibition. (The two terms have specific meanings within the hobby: a vignette is a scene consisting of two to five figures and of relatively modest size; a diorama is a larger scene comprising more than five figures.)

The prospect of embarking on a major diorama can be very daunting indeed. Good dioramas require careful planning, thoughtful composition and a dynamic subject; most of all, they require a lot of time. As most miniaturists like to consider themselves as very methodical, careful artists (some taking pride in claiming that a single stock kit took them months, or in extreme cases even years to paint!), a multiple-figure scene can be pretty intimidating. For this reason far fewer vignettes and dioramas are seen at exhibitions than any of the other main formats.

The diorama presents the modeller with a completely new set of challenges in addition to all those posed by painted stock figures, conversions or scratchbuilts. Apart from all the skills necessary for making and painting the figures, he faces the tasks of designing and modelling a section of terrain or a building in such a way as to emphasize his "story line"; animating and engineering the figures to produce the desired interaction; composing the scene; and of course, the most important problem of all - selecting a suitable and appealing subject.

A good diorama or vignette does not necessarily require a complex "story" - indeed, concentration on conveying a single governing idea is better than the risk of distracting or confusing the spectator's eye; nor does it need a "cast of thousands" - just whatever it takes to tell the story. While action scenes have always been popular (including cavalry charges, duels, and infantry battles), quiet, even introspective scenes can also make a powerful impression. The sombre farewell of a soldier leaving for duty, a toast to victory on the eve of battle, or a defeated general contemplating his past, and future - all these subjects have been most successfully undertaken, and are illustrated in this chapter.

Probably the ultimate challenge is the box diorama. Pioneered by Ray Anderson, and made famous by

Standard bearers can present a major, if seductive problem for modellers. The difficulties of finding the right material from which to make the "colour" itself (in this case, rolled-out Milliput), and the intricate painting of devices and battle-honours (here carefully rendered in enamel paints) are often enough to discourage the faint-hearted. **Adrian Bay's** excellent vignette "Lindsey and Thistlethwayte", depicting two Scots Fusilier Guard officers of the regiment's colour party at the battle of the Alma, 1854, is a fine example of a difficult challenge overcome.

Sheperd Paine (whose box dioramas continue to be among the most acclaimed achievements in military miniature art), the box enables the miniaturist to control every element of his scene. Lighting, perspective, viewing angle, and a variety of other elements can be precisely manipulated by the artist when his model is planned and engineered to fit inside a box - a miniature stage set, whose picture-frame front forms the proscenium arch. Because of the integral problem of sight lines most box dioramas depict indoor or night scenes, where walls or darkness can mask the oblique angles. When done well the box diorama is perhaps the most satisfying of all achievements in miniaturisation.

As most modellers are also amateur historians, many have become near-experts on certain historical periods. They can regale a captive audience with a never-ending litany of military trivia, not to mention descriptions of numerous fascinating projects "soon to be started"....There are indeed an endless number of fascinating stories to be told; the key is to select one that the miniaturist can successfully communicate. When an interesting incident combines with outstanding engineering skill and miniature painting, the result can be sheer magic.

Above:
Based on an Angus McBride painting for Osprey's Men-at-Arms book on the Celts (MAA 158), **Steve Cozad's** extensively reworked *New Hope Design* vignette "Early Transportation" was among the most popular entries at the 1992 California Show. (Photo: Nick Infield)

Left:
There is a wonderful flair and sense of daring in the work of many French modellers, typified by **Herve de Belenet's** "Khmer War Elephant". The brilliantly designed and painted arch, combined with the stunningly rendered elephant, give this piece great impact. Among its honours was a second place in the 1991 Sevres competition. (Photo: Jean-Louis Viau)

Right:
Joe Berton has long been a master of the 54mm vignette, and throughout the 1970s and 1980s his efforts were consistently among the most acclaimed in North American modelling circles.
His entry for the 1988 Chicago Show, "Battle of the Pyramids", captures the excitement of his earlier work. The well-engineered interaction of the two figures – a tricky problem – is the key to its appeal.

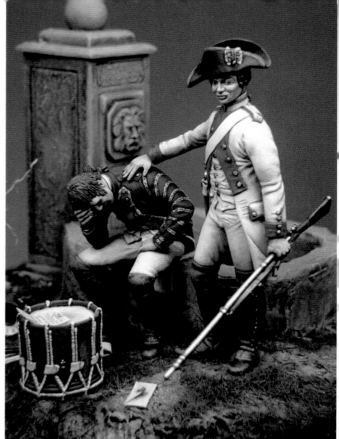

Opposite top left:
Again inspired by the work of a famous illustrator, this time the fantasy artist Frank Frazetta, "Princesse Egyptienne" is a quietly beautiful vignette from the talented hands of France's **Frederic Deroux.** (Photo: Jean-Louis Viau)

Opposite bottom:
Widely renowned as an interior designer, retired U.S.Navy pilot **Roy "Eric" Erickson** is fast developing a reputation as an excellent miniaturist as well, and his vignettes depicting Native Americans have attracted special acclaim. "Wild Meat" captures the drama of the buffalo hunt. Good composition is one key to Eric's success; note the absence of any "dead space" around the central action - important in achieving impact and maintaining viewer focus. (Photo:Nick Infield)

Above & opposite top right:
The multi-talented **Greg DiFranco's** vignettes have added prestigious awards to his trophy case. His well-staged "Dear Jacques", a French 18th century variation on the theme of the "Dear John" letter, was a popular gold medal winner at the 1988 MFCA Show. In 1983 Greg had captured his first major Best of Show at Chicago for his superb Light Brigade vignette,"Flash'd as they turned in air". The figures are extensively reworked *Historex* and *Airfix* kits.(Light Brigade photo: Peter Twist)

Bottom right:
Elephants are always a popular subject at competitions, and French modeller **Philippe Gengembre** won a gold medal at Euro-Militaire in 1991 with his fine "Punic War" scene. (Photo: Jean-Louis Viau)

Left:
Jean Josseau's award-winning vignette "Egypt" is a natural extension of his mastery of the mounted figure, this time combining two riders in breathtaking high-speed combat. The sense of motion which he conveys here, and the unmistakable feeling of imminent peril, make this a particularly impressive work. (Photo:Jean-Louis Viau)

Bottom left:
Quiet, contemplative vignettes are easy to conceive but difficult to carry off well. Commercial artist **Andre Koribanics,** best known for his spectacular *Historex* work in the 1970s and 1980s and equally skilled as a scratch-builder, brilliantly captured the tender poignancy of a soldier's farewell to his little family on leaving for war in this outstanding British Napoleonic vignette, "His Father's Promise". Note again the compact composition, focussing our attention solely on the single governing idea. (Photo:Nick Infield)

Below & right:
Two of the author's creations. "Last Stand at Gandamak" included 27 figures, and depicted the final stand of the 44th Regiment during the disastrous retreat from Kabul in the First Afghan War. One key to good diorama design is tight construction and a well-conceived composition, something attempted in this diorama, which won Best of Show awards at Euro-Militaire and Chicago in 1988. The vignette "The Prisoner" was based upon a late 19th century engraving after R.Caton-Woodville;

again, economy of space was a key element in telling the story, as was the harmony of body language and facial expressions – aggressive impatience in the case of the Highland officer, and surprised anxiety on the part of the Egyptian officer.

Right & opposite page:
A selection of work by **Peter Twist.** The ever-popular three-figure vignette has seldom been handled more boldly than in his MFCA Best of Show winner from 1983, "Cold Steel" - a scratchbuilt 90mm British 4th Foot Waterloo group. The gloomy, lonely elegance of Napoleon's study on Elba was the setting for the eerily contemplative "The Emperor in Exile"; the fixtures and furniture details in this box diorama are mainly doll's house accessories. "La Decouverte Inattendue" captures the romance and drama of the rapier duel, set on the balcony of the distraught cause of the encounter! The carefully crafted balcony is set at just the right angle to open the scene to the viewer; and this box features an extremely effective use of lighting. Since the appearance on the market of fibre-optics, candlelight effects have been added to the essential palette of the box diorama artist.

Below:
Bill Ottinger's depiction of a trio of Napoleonic French Hussars overrunning a line of Bavarian infantry, entitled "Sabres Wicked in their Work", is among his best. Good composition, well-animated figures and a sense of danger made this one of the most popular pieces at the 1984 Chicago Show. (Photo:Bill Ottinger)

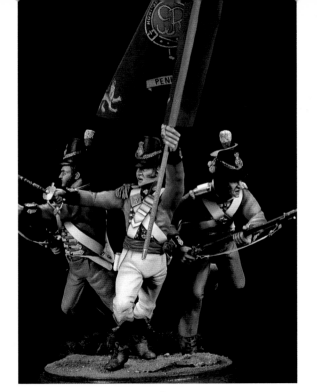

Above:
Two nicely modelled and painted figures of early North American frontier types grace **Victor Hoegarden's** fine piece "Descente de la Riviere". Note the convincingly portrayed water: water effects are one of the classic challenges for the miniaturist, and different materials and techniques are hotly championed wherever modellers meet.
(Photo:Jean-Louis Viau)

Opposite top:
In Shep Paine's 90mm diorama "The Union Forever" the 8th Wisconsin's famous eagle mascot flies defiantly above the National flag as the colour party charge into battle.

Opposite bottom:
Shep's "Roman Riding" is a *Historex*-based conversion featuring a Union Cavalry sergeant demonstrating his equestrian skills to an obviously impressed comrade. The horses and rider are all linked by hidden pins, and supported by a single mounting pin in the right front hoof of one of the horses.

SHEPERD PAINE (U.S.A.)

It is difficult to know where to begin any brief summary of the impact Shep Paine has had on the art of the military miniature. Perhaps using the term "art", to describe what had always previously been considered a hobby based on the collecting and painting of toy soldiers, is in itself the best tribute. Through his many innovations in the realistic painting of miniature figures, in scratchbuilding, plastic modelling, dioramas, and of course his famous "boxes", Shep's impact on the hobby makes that of any other individual modeller seem insignificant. Shep was honoured in the early 1970s as the first MFCA Grand Master, and later received the Chicago Medal, both awards being for sustained excellence in military miniature art. While it can be argued that there are modellers today who can paint and sculpt as well as Shep, it is also certain that without his influence many of those same modellers might now be collecting postage stamps instead!

Shep's ability to tell a story through a combination of excellent engineering, construction, modelling and painting, but especially through meticulously planned and carefully executed composition - or "stage managing", as he calls it - is dazzling, as can be seen here in his photographs of just a few of his many show-stoppers. Sheperd Paine is a true Grand Master in every sense of the words.

Left:
One of Shep's best 54mm vignettes is "The Promotion", depicting the traditional wetting down of the newly earned stripes of an Imperial Guard Grenadier sergeant.

Below:
One of Shep's most famous boxes is "To a Fair Wind and Victory", depicting Nelson's toast at the dinner for his officers on the eve of the battle of Copenhagen. Note the skilful use of lighting, and the remarkable details added to create the feel of authenticity.

"A Stillness at Appomattox" is a rarely seen box diorama from 1988. The dejection clearly evident in the face of General Robert E.Lee as he awaits the arrival of General Grant is very moving. The staging here is particularly good, as the two "supporting actors" are animated to tell the viewer of the imminent arrival of the other key player in the drama. In work like this the master miniaturist can tell a story as eloquently as the great 19th century genre painters.

In "Assault on Redoubt No.10 at Yorktown" Shep illuminated the entire scene with tiny red grain-of-wheat lights in the barrels of the firing muskets, achieving an astonishing effect of "frozen movement".

FINAL THOUGHTS

One of the most inspiring things about being involved in military miniature art is the eagerness with which modellers share their ideas, techniques and enthusiasm for their work. In the ten years since I attended my first competition I have never once met a miniaturist unwilling to talk about his or her work, or to explain how he or she achieved a particularly striking effect. In fact, of course, a twinkle comes into the eye of the proud modeller when he sees his efforts appreciated by his peers, and the admiring bafflement of his colleagues is music to his ears as he prepares to share his solution to the problem overcome. The result of this generosity and openness has been an improvement in the quality of the work being done by all – as the miniatures illustrated in this book so vividly demonstrate.

Much credit for helping to bring about this renaissance must go to the organizers of the major miniature competitions and exhibitions, particularly **Euro-Militaire** at Folkestone, England; the **Sevres Competition** in Paris; and the two major exhibitions in the United States – the **Chicago Show,** and the **MFCA Show** at Valley Forge, Pennsylvania. By providing such a congenial and supportive environment for miniaturists these events have been a major factor in shrinking the modelling world and lowering its frontiers. The advent of the World Model Soldier Federation, and plans for a tri–annual international military miniature Expo, are a direct result of the friendships formed among the world's modellers. Still, it is the miniaturists themselves who are the true stars of the show – through their hard work and skill they have helped raise their hobby to a new level of art; and they have put on a show worth watching!

Adrian Bay's "Colour-Sergeant Munro, VC, 93rd Highlanders, 1857", a virtually scratchbuilt 54mm conversion painted with enamels.